THROUGH THE YEARS

also by Ricardo Quinones

North/South: The Great European Divide
(U Toronto P 2016)

Fringes
(39 West Press 2015)

Finishing Touches
(39 West Press 2014)

A Sorting of the Ways: New and Selected Poems
(39 West Press 2011)

Roberta and Other Poems
(39 West Press 2011)

Erasmus and Voltaire: Why They Still Matter
(U Toronto P 2010)

Dualisms: The Agons of the Modern World
(U Toronto P 2007)

Foundation Sacrifice in Dante's "Commedia"
(Penn State UP 1994)

The Changes of Cain: Violence and the Lost Brother
(Princeton UP 1991)

Mapping Literary Modernism: Time and Development
(Princeton UP 1985)

Dante Alighieri
(Twayne 1979; updated revised edition 1998)

The Renaissance Discovery of Time
(Harvard UP 1972)

THROUGH THE YEARS

POEMS BY

Ricardo Quinones

39 WEST PRESS
Kansas City, MO
www.39WestPress.com

39 WEST
P R E S S

Copyright © 2010 by Ricardo Quinones

All rights reserved. No part of this book may be reproduced, scanned, or distributed in any printed or electronic form, including information storage and retrieval systems, without permission. Please do not participate in or encourage piracy of copyrighted materials in violation of the author's rights. Please purchase only authorized editions.

First Edition: November 2010

ISBN: 978-0-615-41696-0

Library of Congress Control Number: 2010940188

This book is a work of fiction. Names, characters, places, dates, and incidents are products of the author's imagination, or are used fictitiously, satirically, or as parody. Any resemblance to actual persons, living or dead, business establishments, events, or locales is entirely coincidental.

10 9 8 7 6 5 4 3 2

Design & Layout: j.d.tulloch
Front & Back Cover Paintings: Astrid Preston

39WP-01A

For Roberta, Sam, Ben and Josh

Profuse thanks to Astrid Preston for the use of her two magical paintings, "Azure Blue Sky" and "Above the Imperial Palace," for the front and back covers respectively.

CONTENTS

PART 1

The first thing out tramping	3
Newspapers	5
Aggressively, Kansas	7
SoCal: A Sorting of the Ways	9
Wallet Poems I	12
Why Do Grown Men Weep?	17
Uncles	19

PART 2

Gilbert Paoli	23
Esau (as spoken by the man himself)	25
Wintertime Sun	27
Wallet Poems II	29
Domestic Arrangements	34
Domestic Interrogative	35

PART 3

Architectura (After the Statue at the Bargello)	39
A Woman Dead	41
Photograph of an Aged Woman Amidst Her Iris	43
Atonements	44
An American Writer	46
Wallet Poems III	48
Desert Bloom	55
A Glass of Deep Red Wine	57
Wanderers	59
Oil and Water	61
I want to go back again	63

PART 1

The first thing out tramping
Is to roust a sleeping stick,
Good for knocking at trees
Or golf about the leaves.
Sight down a shot or two,
Ward off critters and feral things
Club to smithereens.
One that comes ready to hand,
Doughty and bluff at the end,
Tapered smooth at the grip,
A natural extension of self,
And a pendant part of striding,
Like crunching deep in crusted snow.

Newspapers

Why do we read the papers,
A world in which we are only part at home?
A ritual of reconnection
After night's salt sailings,
A national debriefing time
Of stewing at the village well
Or grousing at the kitchen table.
A daily diet of madness
Of verification and some acclaim
Or is it simply a short attention span
The solidarity of the commonplace.
Where nothing strays,
Yet everything stays—like the evening news—
At a level of depression,
Like radon on the cellar stairs.

It's a glaring register of fact
—Yes, that describes what did happen,
That was you with the digits of age—
Undeniable and inadmissible
Mug-shots taken on trust.
One-by-one they stand there
Line items with no veto.
Yet facts unstoried can't possibly add up.
For this we take to dreams,
Or Shakespeare's last plays.
They bring back tales and fearing times,
Wrongings real and true,
Fittings that we hazard to recall.

That's why we read the papers.
It's a gathering time,
A way of filling up
The useless and the random,
Collectibles to no purpose,
Horrors to no event.

They all must go someplace,
If only to dream's seven doors
With only one bullet in the gun
Yet these doors are corridors that meet
Tunneling and furnishings found
You only need to plunge down one
—that's all the steps it takes—
To plunder room and begetting room.

Aggressively, Kansas

Who's on call for Kansas
With its subtleties of sunken rage?
Where in the men's locker room
Signs in hand-written scrawl
Chasten the brazen and the bold
"Others are tired of your parts
Hanging out all over."
Modesty cloths spread over sprawl.
Concealments that bring to the fore.

>   Frost is on the window, drift is on the pane
>   Frost will go and come again.
>   Write with the finger, write with the pen
>   Frost will run and come again.

Picket fences are guardian rails
Masterpieces of daggered inflection
Swords pointed up, blood humiliation
Containing sledge that won't recede
All sufficiencies of evil within

>   Frost is on the window, drift is on the pane
>   Frost will go and come again.
>   Write with the finger, write with the pen
>   Frost will go and come as rain.

Like God's lightning it shivered the earth
And instantly severed the chord.
Oh unminding twittering squirrel
Caught in an effigy of prayer
—Oh hart that pants—
A red-tail hawk squandered your last meal.
With talons like manacles it straddled its prey,
Between the Union and Strong Hall,
The lunch-time crowd cordoned itself,
Confounded by that great event.

Who could dislodge him from his rightful seat,
That broad forehead and rigid stare,
The natural instinct of grand design,
Flocked in self-determining fate,
Pinioning its primal erotic mate.
It plunges its beak but to withdraw
Like dangling pasta the smoking entrails.

      Frost is on the window, drift is on the pane
      Frost will go and come again.
      Write with the finger, write with the pen,
      Frost will run and come again.

So pick it up bleeding Kansas,
Where no one catches a word on the wing,
Baffled by any thrown-out fling.
Work that line of words at risk,
Like a bullfighter all sheen and piffled color,
Whose body is bent like a fiddler's bow
At the mound of groined exposure,
Each time, each sand, each roar
Taking the chance of contact direct
The sacerdotal function of respect.

      Frost is on the window, frost is in the grain.

SoCal: A Sorting of the Ways

"All people are the same,"
Breezing she goes over her bubbly,
"Oh no they're not,"
Passing on the fly I let out,
With which I am glad to say
Even my masseuse agreed
Though she doubled down on diversity

Thus began my recent run
Of California skirmish
My adopted native land
Once again my chest hollow sinks
At the latest gush of fabled wealth
Flotillas of pricey models
Preen as they parade
Through every street and strip
Barracuda-eyed and snub-nosed
Contoured additions to the terrain

Down that sink-hole cycle
I did not need the vocal brand
"STK PRFT"
On a Bemmer tooling by
"I am glad you spent it dear," I think
"But need you advertise the haul?
Wasn't older wealth more discreet?
They didn't shower in the street."
Democratic ease and sufficient opulence
Was how Whitman wanted it
And particularly better
If the getter knew how it was gotten
Or was somewhat philanthropic.

My heart jumped
When barely an hour later
An apparition rounded the verge
Of my condo complex road
A retired couple—no down-and-outers they—
She quite pert in her synthetic whites
And he slim trim and neatly tucked
Carrying a pick-spade in one
And in the other hand a veggie bag
Something had clearly turned round
The tunings of southern Orange County.

You can bet my converse was eager
Magi never met an equal joy
A communal garden they were tending
And he rattled off the shades of lettuce
Iceberg, romaine, escarole and more
Like Bottom I was delirious
With sweet peas and snap peas
Keep ringing them up, please, I implored
20 x 20 plots of land-fill
With water twenty dollars a year,
I thought we were back with FDR
Pilfering was of no account
They had a renewable resource
And didn't need what they didn't have.

Such sorting of the ways:
Diagonal from these municipal plots
Students zoom up in sporty cars
And uncontrollable apparel
Parents wait their wagons throbbing
Yet symphonists still master on
With brows of concentrated fervor.

My own way stepped far back then
To our own "Victory" garden
When through hot summers of WWII
Over the Lehigh River bridge
I carried our baskets of produce
Hoards for winter storage
Festive salads on our Italian table
Those medleys of color and chord.

That very eve of the big Spring change
The crescent first moon
Hung phosphorescent and alone
Except for Venus
Minding the ladle
As my friend Rik explained
Whose growth on his prostate
Is to be cut come Monday prime.

Wallet Poems I

1.
Wallet poems you carry with you,
All folded up with proper care,
Like sheets in the hallway closet,
Like books perched high on a chair.

Like sheets their use is private,
Like books they're read alone.
Release m their confinements,
Distend their wings in air.
Like sheets, like books, you'll find
Matters sufficient for play—
The common places of the everyday.

2.
Don't be harsh, my dear wife
Against those circling rings.
Love handles are gifts of age
And the fruits of a happy life.

Like trees they only add to core
The bark where I take hold,
When in our striving love
You come to ask for more.

3.
Mirrors are terrible hosts,
Not knowing left from right
Like newcomers to the coast
Who argue with the setting sun,
All misdirected in its run
Even shadowy things, like hair astray
Can cause considerable dismay.

Did not Sartre devise his theories
When sighting his back in a mirror
Believed it belonged to another?
Such tricks do reflections play.
Our minds must steady to shun confusion,
Enact a concentration of form.
Yet even that requires a focus,
Sapping strength of single purpose.

How can we be two souls in one?
That is an enterprise of some exertion.
Like mirrored misconstruals,
Like the acting part
Struggle inheres in all we do,
To stay the one while knowing double,
Eschew forlornness and dread
And bring to mouth our daily bread?

4.
I hate the extensions of winter,
Thirty days run on of thirty below.
They're like irrationalities of sound,
A bellowing mutt, a slamming door
Or temblors that won't die down.

There's something willful in extension,
That dogged persistence of prolong,
The same thing on and on.
Less is more where infinity's the scope,
Something arguing a quietness of style.
Isn't once and done good enough?
Why pull from the bag
All that bric-a-brac stuff,
Down to each everlasting chug?
Infinity is undone by an addition of one.
Infinity is always the same.
But one is a nonesuch,
And that is unique
And everlasting just as much.

5.
Pillow talk will land us all in jail,
Those amorphic utterances of grunt and twist,
Argotic grimaces of vengeful thrust,
No need for words where gestures suffice.

The genius of love absolves us there
Turning the gleam of aggressive intent
To stilled thoughts, quiet and touching care
And thus declares us innocent by event.

6.
Everything we take has its toxic side,
Like those pills that consume half a line,
Whatever we ingest or take bed,
Residuals of remorse, of bottom, of head.

Only our love, my dear, carries no blame.
From bottom to top and back to bottom again,
From day to night, from night to ringing day,
It touches all points, remarkably the same.

7.
How could she possibly be a lover,
Who licks those scars of slighted merit?

It's wrong to love another more than self,
Why love that which loves not you?
Unreturned calls that don't measure up,
Deliberations of avoidance clear,
From people you'll find not of your sphere.

But that sadly will not matter
When image of the mind takes hold,
The need to quell that which wants not you,
An imperial instinct to control
That converts to prey hunter and bold.

Love cannot be more nor less than self
But rather seeks that which has no end,
Magnetic drawings of tumultuous embrace,
Those things that bring us face to face.

8.
We don't choose the day, the day chooses us.
Like quarterbacks returned from long time out.
Who is to know why things didn't mesh,
An unreckoned lurch, baggage all spilling.
Poor teaming, poor timing, certainly not merit?
Head and heart geared to purposes diverse.

And now in age the truth comes back,
Beyond deserts an in-pouring,
Ease of place offers such squaring,
One not unrelated to merit.
He paid hard for acquisitions of the way,
The accumulated graces, the exactions of delay.

9.
A large couch is heaven's treasure
Supporting the ways we work,
Flat-out, reclined, or legs akimbo
It does not matter as to worth.
Capacious in the TV room

Where three can sit per view,
It's best used as a love-boat,
Where I first toppled you.

10.
A poem may be like poke,
All rectangular and bulk,
Until it sets to jostling,
Like child in womb
All bend and flurry
Of arms and angles
Messing to take place,
Bringing to force
Recognitions that stagger
Revelations, a face.

Coda
And am I now in Ilyria?
It was all so hard finding.
The riven bark, the circling rind,
Things dying, things new born.
And how is it not Ilyria?
Music at every turn,
A strolling buzz, lolling airs—
And the humming,
All listening to yourself out loud.

Why Do Grown Men Weep?

Why are grown men weepers?
Not late-hour TV hucksters.
But Camus, Naipal and surely others,
Caustic, who write standing up.

It has something to do with fathers,
Now long gone but signaling wrongs.
A single concavity of space
That's present like an amputation.
Definitely a man's thing,
Not like women who flood on occasion,
These weep on no occasion at all.
You might as well bawl at open air
Or decades of emptiness consumed.
Ampler meanings are required here.

With Freud some dark event intruded
When sons throttled the expiring King.
Far gone and muddled for our story
Its implications still are grave,
Pointing to prevailing conditions:
These natures non-communicative
Awkward to urinate side-by-side,
The clogged strengths of muffled truths
And inner beasts they daren't surrender.

There's still offense and injury keen.
Think of Samuel Johnson bare-headed
Absorbing the penitential rain
All day where he did his father wrong.
But such contrition is extreme
A glowing gift earned by few.
Baroque repentance may be forgone
If this one thing is kept in mind:
Tit-for-tat will care for that.

Compensation calls for equal shares
What sons did fathers in turn is theirs.

These considerations may be tabled.
They are things done, incidents of scale.
We are calling up things that never were,
Contrary to event or what was inferred.
That's why grown men weep,
Watchmen of their fathers inert,
It's from pictures in the mind
Missed conviviality of accord,
Something never to be given,
Something stayed as men with kind
Not past times to reopen
But times not given to return.

Fathers' gifts are sleights-of-hand.
What's not there counts the most.
We picture them with arms of bounty,
Hams and sacks and bottled things,
Or perched for dust at a cowboy movie
Or circled with chums at the shore,
And we join in with voice elated
"Isn't this the cat's own balls!"
And they all hulking nod for sure.

We can never be truly convivial.
One perishes by the other's gain,
All those shiftings of generational weight
Are staffings out by the trail.
Perhaps some meeting at Resurrection gate,
But that's past ours to paint
And that's why tears assail grown men.
They understand how all things end.
Never to be righted, and beyond recall.

Uncles

The luckiest thing for a little girl
Is to have gigantic uncles
Such as guard the approaches
Not letting any cut-throats in
Nor handy-dandy hooligans
Let alone some fairy prince.

Boxes they bring of brightened desire
With secret drawers and brassy knobs
Beads and brooches they contain
All spilling like sparkles of fire.

They pitch and throw her about
In widening circles of willing dare
Circus performers of beaten skill
Never held such certain hands
Or felt their swings so secure.

Later they will tender her first drink
A martini mixed with swirl
Held up to the light and sipped
To the delight of any lady-like girl.

Watcher wardens of the place
Designers of adventure free
Just think what our world would be
Without such hands to sculpt our space.

Yet, come as come it must, cancer,
The physics of other inscrutable ills.
But that does not diminish what's begun
Guardians now mounted on walls
Still residents of the place
Claiming new generations
Substances that cohere

Stabilities of choice
With speech that does not err
An openness to engage
Without a flicker of fear.

PART 2

Gilbert Paoli*

We should all be made into bronze
And cast as Olympian superb
Models of healthy aspire
Fronting the Institut Pasteur.

But in bronze there is no quick,
That paper-weight of imposing mass
No saving breath or sweat in pores
Wearing a walkman of containment
A blinding to whatever occurs.

Quick is what we had
In LA after the War
Crescendo, Ciro's, LaRue,
That was before '72,
When the hippies came to sit
And occupied the Strip.

No master's hand, no grand design,
Inadvertence unschooled
Conveyed its own gathering art
Beyond our skills to contrive,
Moments too happy to know
Because you were the moment,
And by its own inverted light
The moment was you.

Not a series of moments,
Rather a texture of commotion,
Call it an epoch, a swirl,
Or simply a snag in the line.
The only art they could own
Was that of marvelous display.
But this much we can secure,
They had their world in their time,
With no sense of being passed by.

Like a long happy, lucky love
Never a thought as to end,
But simple vibrations to a feel,
Except for some mindfulness
Exalted by a judgment fit
Calling to all listen,
"Never such times again."

And just as certainly
As market's overnight plunge
It was gone from sight
A strange relinquishment
As of a borrowed thing,
Or an old adhesive's rip
That preciousness in time
Not to be found in art
Only the bending circles of smoke
And receding ash that old men stoke.

Gilbert Paoli was a prominent restaurateur in the period described; he was also the model for Health outside the Institut Pasteur in Paris.

Esau
(as spoken by the man himself)

Heavy-lifting is the hard-hat part
Then comes some alec with a tart remark
Like dropping in for the kill
On a cross-word puzzle
With only a few blanks to fill
Or some brigand
Vaulting debonaire
Breathes over your solitaire
And then strides off
Like Charles Darwin
Or Achilles over the asphodel.

Then I go wild
Against God's scales
It's like someone getting mad
At you for getting mad
But I was there first I wish to state
That was my land
Don't I have my rights
The pioneer, the first comer
Not these prodigal Johnnies
Waltzing through the daffadowndillies
At some cherry-picker's ball

Get smart is turnabout
Here all is for the play
Now by device I leave some spaces
And watch them bloat
To plunk down the pimp
Or, fatting them with puzzle pieces
I smile to watch them jump the fit
That's jollifying those tadpoles
Just ducky that vie en rose
It's called keeping on your toes.

Now I get the meaning of sin
Mocking God's plan
Chuckling over small triumphs
It's a withering within.
Wear a fish-hook with happy style
Return smile for plastered smile
With a better hand
Fold before the bettings started
Warrant a petty insight piercing smart
Knowing it's far off the mark
With scissor-kicks of injured merit
I play out the trickster's part
Not joying in another's delight
But trading score-cards of despite

Wintertime Sun

I have a romance
With the wintertime sun
I scuttle indoor plans
To sit all hunched in its glaze
My covered pate cranes
Like seagulls lining the shore
All driven to front the glow.
It doesn't beat down from above
With blinding garish blaze
Where you have to raise your hand
To fend off the glare,
But forehead to forehead straight
Translucent like pearly light
Behind a silken screen
Expends its brightness everywhere.

So different from everything
Of which it is a part
It's an earnest light
A willingness that's ingrained
An economy of appeal
Like words that hold to their mold
On their purposes intent
And won't let go
Blotting out all intrusions—
Blithering TV commercials,
Radio traffic reports
Repetitions without end
The Dionysian Hollywood stars
And their celebrity touts—
Dead before they even begin
Thus laboring to perish from within.

I'll take this time, this season
With all its shortness of hours
O wintertime sun
You've saved the best for last

Wallet Poems II

1. "Strippins"
I met an old enemy
Now defunct of mind
It's hard to find advantage
In such catastrophes of kind
Encasements
Like when we were kids
Fishing at the "strippins"
With twig and pin antwine
Waters black and cold
When all the takings have been mined

2.
Sight unaware of seeing.
That's no matter for fright.
Other systems work this way
Our innards carry on
Without our say-so or espying.
When we know what they're about
Things are not all right.
When they clamor for attention
There's a reason for complaint.
This must recommit us—
Sight is best when not in view,
Exactly as at the beginning
Jibings without that dither
Like Willie Mays in center
All our senses pulling one way
Arm out-stretched, catch at sight
One-on-one, back-to-back
Then, and only then, god-like.

3.
Wallet poems are light in purse
Like bills
Mere tokens in verse
Of the bigger stuff around
Like assets banking otherwheres.
They are just the gleanings
The interest earned
Grabbings that abound.
Neither ejected members
Nor bills of state
But happy little wanderings
Sleepers doting on the sly
Without extra weight
Good to fill a pinch or two
And in that way carry their freight.

4.
There's an emergence in verse.
Acknowledgment of what is just
Working its way with blessed shoes
Past contention's barriers
And over carrion's to-do's.

5.
His mind has taken to hiding.
He has given up trying to decipher
Its cramped and ragged writing
Like a heart beat flattened out
Like the kids gone to Florida
Where nobody's seen again.

By practiced notes to himself
And other furtive ruses
He labors to rehearse what it was
He thought he knew
Like a child wobbling to walk—
Before relinquishing the tangle
And putting down where it says he is.

**6. Geastich li l'olam (I entwine you forever)
  from an Hebrew wedding prayer**
My head in your crotch,
Yours in mine ensconced
Thus all sleep enpretzelled
Topsy-turvy, toes upcurled
Like children, like twins in womb
Not forbidden
But by Good Words enjoined,
"One body, one flesh"
Add to them "one mind"
And they might show how married love
Is fully entwined.

7.
Your hair all flaxen and afly
Your cheeks burnished as autumn
Your smile running to broad as the moon.
You did not know love was such a harvester

8.
Don't blame tautology.
That legacy of botched survey
Is a roundabout along the way
Making unsure direction's flow
Alternating either way "get" with "go."

There's a substance that precedes knowing
What's to do get's done by going
We can grasp the map's markers
Only after marching's started
Dust in the eyes makes vision smarter.

This hitch so orders our things
We only make love when love is in us
We only make do when already so-so
Waltzing conveys the steps of the dance—
Knowing is not an incoming beam—
But what comes from our projecting screen.—

A circle is not that vicious
Just making sure we touch all the bases
—a purpose that governs—
Bringing "home" before "run"
Making us end where we've begun.

9.
I called out "Go to Hell"
To my Parkinson's last night
—Stalking the table
Running shot after shot—
Mingled with other abuse,
"You miserable dimwit, you"

But it just stood waiting
A bit stepped back
Chalking its cue—
Expecting my next mistake

10.
The most libidinous thing
(By me most certainly drawn out)
Is to hear my wife tell
Of her past lovers and love.

Sizes, I'm afraid
Attentiveness for sure
Ineptitudes of a few
Some dangerous rendez-vouz.

Her compliance is reluctant
Only to set the record straight
While I
Operate under constraint
As if it were my immediate stake.

O happy, happy love
What arrows you throw
Not only bolts of pictured fire
But other tinglings there
—As bow takes to quiver—
All conspiracies of desire.

Domestic Arrangements

Lines drawn in the sand
Are meekly futile, largely offensive
Like pre-marital agreements
Divorced from the start
Legalized principles of discord
Invitations to infringement
The "mine" and "thine" of mediated blight
Like fridges with halves consigned,
Like markets readied for flight.

Something abject here took hold
Mechanical rules of the house
Boundaries turned outside in
Guns trained on their own,
What really should be a DMZ
A duty-free zone of intent,

Where we wander as we might
Like crossing the street
At a scramble corner
Without need of light
Telling us when to go, to stop,
Or keep to the right.
Such things are needed
But not by regulation.
They come down from love
Unmuddled by calculation.
Married love has more to mean
Than merely rules of self-regard
Its great task is just to be
Eager expectation
And first morning's sight
Not turned away, squiney-eyed
By severe applications of right.

Domestic Interrogative

As an instrument of blunt force
A question is a remark.
It might not shut any door
In a momentous, final manner,
Nor seem a summons to the witness stand
Like being called to give a reason.
It's a domestic interrogative,
As, "Did you do the thing you went to do?"

The point-blank question direct
Is hardly aggressive, maybe captious
That's not what puts us out,
It's the normal insulating effect,
As if it were ours alone to perform
And not that of the questioner.
The burden all pushed to one side,
Not that from which the pushing comes.
As if only one were to be remitted
While the fulcrum of the world
Sends its gore point to the other.

It does scare up enormous shifts
Packing us off to other inquisitions,
Did it have to come to point direct,
Could not more have been said,
"Was it a successful trip, my dear?"
Or, "I hope the wait wasn't too long?"
More like an out-stretched arm,
Beholding a structure of design,
Circumambient and refined,
Not the stiff shoulder shove
That frisks away the figment of love.

PART 3

Architectura
(After the Statue at the Bargello)

Isn't it odd
That architectura is a woman
When the bestrident male
Might better intend the epitome's mold
Like the bronzes of Riace
At which women have been known to weep
To see in living form
Their dreams of young athletic grace
And leaping spirits not tied by weight.

Back on earth their arms athwart
Show a readiness of response
Equal to any situation
Even their ribbed torsos
Like jutting palazzo walls
Or a bulldog in tow
Clearly bring to mind
The Mart of jowly Chicago
Or the squat rotary phone
Now happily replaced by the roam.

Hard to ignore the tall ones
That set all the cities vying
Those stretched sky-walks
Wonders of man-child's intent
Not very subtle in their aspiring
Burrowing upwards to the firmament.

Such agitation is not woman's thing
Imagine suffering The Ring.
No, no! That Architectura is feminine
Has to do with a dignity of holding
An arm that beckons
In refined enfolding
Alignments of embrace
A tendency to assuage
Solicitations of care
Mitigations of malaise
Giving us to know our belonging there.

But the billowing adumbrations
Her draping folds of stony dress
Impart other directions as well
Like Ariadne's string of clues
They are weavings to no clearing
They landscape a journey
Of mountain passes
Throwing some wrinkle in time
Part Circe's mischief
Part Penelope's rule.
All they require is a willingness to sustain
With no turning back after the first foot-fall.

These circlings round of arm and gown
Are openings that astound
Containments of space
That bring to hatch the warmth of the sun
And yes
Apollo fronting the lineaments of the race.

A Woman Dead

I hardly knew what it meant
When I heard she was dead.
Nor did the Episcopal service help
Meager in its needy celebration.
Better a cadenza, a fandango
Feet stomping, glasses broken
Even a flat Western drawl,
"She's stiff as nail in a wall."

Three more famous deaths
Left her in their paper traces;
First, Longdon, that winner of races
Now surpassed by Shoe, Pinky and Baze;
Then Vietnam's pot-shot artist
Who strangely bore Walt Whitman's name;
Then Kid Gavilan, my boyhood champ,
Showy with his bolo extravaganza
Ended shining shoes in Castro's Havana

But these are only buttons of fame
The crust but not the bread
She was not made of that stuff
Oh the movements of this friend
Her walk was so fluid
You swore her knees did not bend.

Only rage disfigured her motion
That of women abandoned by mates.
Begun by her father, of course,
Who decamped when she was budding
Not helped by a mother who hates.

No wonder her line was war,
The Gestalt of, but war all the same,
And dropped her Southern double name
Or occasionally fell for the allure
Of a younger woman's flair.

She never engendered
No robin red breast popping seed
But neither did she bear indifference—
Letters not answered, calls not returned—
Her responses were immediate
And broke from the ends of her veins.

And so one made room
Allowing that fluidity of motion
To come to a flowering of grace
Another bright whisk in the particularities of place.

Photograph of an Aged Woman Amidst Her Iris

Nature grants no respite;
In its dispatches
Holding back is not the way
High embarrassments are thus engendered
Like pudenda laying bare
Or all those swords strapping there
Those things not to be shunned
By an aged woman amidst her iris
Whose growths overtop her quite.

Still she holds to all that splay
The grit that photos convey
Her head slightly weighted
Weavings down from her thinning hair
Forming an oval of studied suggestion
On her breasts own sagging combine
A darkening that's sure to smite
An end in sight
A mandala of hooded grief
An amulet of offered speech
Hands enclosed in a tableau of prayer
Coupling a dome of thatched embrace
All that Mary—virgin and mother—
Was brought to bring
A knowing that's biological and spare.

Atonements

The hero drags a punishing sack
An extremity of grace to atone
Just enough to blunder his step
Or alter his pace to stuttering effect.

Great storage is its own betraying
A club foot, a lump on the back
Those partners in pain
Burdens necessary to assume
Misdirected, distracted, untamed.

That is why he's many years gone
The penalty is actually an urging
A forced uprising that extends the run
A necessary span to permit an unfolding.

    Odysseus doubled his time
    For barking his name
    Dante an equal amount
    For pulling the Pope's tail
    And Shakespeare, mighty Shakespeare
    (Wagner is beyond repair)
    More sinned against than sinning
    But sinning nonetheless
    How else explain such injured exclaim
    Before relenting he forgave.

But it is not the extent of space
Nor the travel of years that matters
They're only numbers that shadow
The shouldering burden he carries.
Before what he knew as possible only
He now hails home by bone and damaged bearing.

Driven by a strange excess
To arrive at his just intent
Those declarations he intended to make
Now come unbidden
With nothing else to attend
Fronting the force of the winds
And down the accumulated years

The American Writer

Not all return from battle
Not all imbalance is restored.
Hemingway comes to mind, our native son,
All shoulder, strap and sword
A first-rate man acting as third,
Straddling legs, and arms extended,
A barreling master of bar-room brawl,
Of combat patrols and wars he won.
How could that man consent to lie,
Repeal at source language he crafted
And the stern truths he tended?

Don't blame that man for lordly claims
Even stupidities of vile demeanor.
His wounds went back too far,
Parcels detained, garments derided,
Abusings that came to stay
Like a field of error acquiring mass
Determining a line of raucous behavior.
Perhaps he no longer wished to give of his time,
He who already had given so much.
Straitened so between two lives,
Observed and always observing.

Make no mistake there was consentment,
A frontier audaciously breached,
Like owing oneself another drink,
Or straying into a punishing car,
Steel shoved to the head of the mouth.
There is in death a skilled inclining,
A willful phantom of abandon,
That we can know but not determine,
The sudden freedom of letting go.

Now we can know those figures he mounted.
That long-lunging, harrowing regale
Whose gleam he trafficked downwards,
Throwing back time eventful and free,
Claiming his place with splendid cast,
No stumbling slippage or wincing shame,
Where no shark comes to strip his gain.
Just Ernest, Cal Lowell and their originals in crime
The Kid named Billy, other mountebanks sublime.
No scraps for salvage from death's passing trains.
A teeming wildness breaks from their veins

Children of Luck they lived to wager
Chancing a grandeur of living fame
Now at this moment of final time
Let it pour down like cleansing rain

Wallet Poems III

1.
Scooting along the airport concourse
In a tightly-fitted cart
It's not wrong to give thumbs-up
To those who trundle along
Even those who pass on walk-ways
To slightly quicken their pace.

It's like rolling down a diamond lane
With open country in sight
Past the braking singles
The only things to balk the flow
Are looky-lou's who go too slow
Or cars not keeping to the right.

Such exalted riding
Should offer no offense
To gods—or other-worldly beings—
It's so small a recompense
For all the vengeful bolts
That struck my buoyant striding.

2.
"Love ensued
Followed by marriage
Followed by children."

Such matters, irreversibly stated
Are too much in a line,
Like pictures in a family album
They follow from a start.
Why not the reverse?
I've seen children
Followed by marriage
With love bailing from behind.

We cannot return omelet to the egg
Or start a scaffold from the top
Even back-tracking a home run
While it flies in cricket
Is in baseball clearly out
Bringing all things to a stop
But change of course in living
Argues an effort of trust
What works one way

The other can bestow as much
Callings are not bases
To be touched in order given
Or numbers in serial pursuit
But buildings-up of fullness
With abundance sought en route.

3.
Who can endure the Holocaust
Convoke it with measured tone?
Its victims are still not counted
So do such evils rumble on.

Or like Mandela emerge
From long time in jail
With intellect in firm hold
And beyond all righteous zeal
Forego vengeance's appeal.

But our tallies here must alter
History with the indifference
Of a blackjack dealer
Has shuffled a nowhere hand
Disgust, weariness and grim reason
Are our cards to bundle
Little there to make a stand.

But even amidst such ashes
We can certainly keep
As Luther did often require
Well beneath martyrdom
Or sanctity's fire
Our home place just as well
A steadfastness where we daily dwell.

4.
Obits have acquired some style
They're much in view and amply read
Occupying more than half a page
With gleaming photos riding high
They seem to wave as you go by
And kill you with a smile.

Even by-lines are provided
Like signatures on works of art
Nothing is left outside
Not even cause of death
—from once we used to smart—
Although some, like pancreatic cancer
Still bring occasion for fear.
For AIDs there's always partners
Or complications left untold
While divorced mates are placed on hold.

Nothing like it used to be
With dank columns all in a row
One on top of other
Like cemeteries in Spain
Intercalations of corpses
Families all together run
Even the borders dressed in black
They hewed to the basics
Not things we were anxious to learn
They called it propriety
The stance of things held private
Not meant for public display.

5. "Festina Lente"
Married love moves slowly by delay
It sheds garments one by one
—no rampageous clumpings on the floor
Nor cries of havoc like declaring war—
And puts away all in detail
Or hangs neatly to keep the press.
It brushes teeth and removes eyes
And might replace a toilet roll
That casual sense of innings to spare—
Those things in store.
Then proceeds to always find more
Of the gestures of love—
Perpetually the same—
That perpetually restore.

(I do wish she would move it, though)

6. Silence
Silence is not a non-event.
It's not even remote
Most likely it's resolute
Hemispheric and snug
Like an old blanket
Up-close with a touch of fuzz
—Satin is much too sheen—
A containment that's domed
Permeating all.

It's a presence to be known
Even carrying weight
Something we can step through
Like stalking rooms
After a quake
Or cleaving mortuary gloom.

Even where there's noise
Silence can still be heard
Choppers don't matter much
Nor the blowers I thought were banned.
Some dominance of the larger sphere
Beamings in the air
And sendings down
That only ask our waiting.
Like solitude
It follows the promptings of mind.
Hence all those pourings of sound.

7. Camera Shy
There's something wrong about pictures,
Those texts of staring truth
Are figures that we're bettered by,
Ingrained instances of rebuke.

A photograph is pictured fate
A consumed fixing of regard
Telling why natives are camera shy,
Where every suerte is malign.

A larger problem is the evil eye,
And objections to the double view
That makes you think you're looking at you,
Like seeing your own sight,
Or asking why thoughts come as they do,
Disablings of sense in a very basic way,
Making us stare
While watching ourselves being there.
A dubious dubbing or a split screen,
Like someone else taking your name.

Three reasons good enough
To make us pause when pictures go round.
But there is something that defies recoil,
Some urging to our stare,
Something so relentless
Like tracking paws in the snow.
Those very same three—
Truth, fate and double view—
Compilings of high stories
Tell the dramas of you.

8.
There is a song
I hear the Cubans sing
How the flowers weep
And other such inordinate things

To hear Omara's song
You know the streets she's roamed
And even Ibrahim comes along
To count his woes and ways
But I want to say
Adding a bit to their trouble
You don't need the flowers
I can contribute to the treble
Believe me my baggage is full
—My cause is great—
I glisten too
As much as the flowers would do.

Even as I limp along
I harbor those tears;
They are, as I now know,
The springs and source of song.

9. End Notes

There's an avarice in poetry
Accumulations of the hoard
A gross gluttony of the heart
Throwing eyes over the board
A numbering through of sheaves
Like tallied bills in hand
Or mail clutched in foreign lands
A lust that marks its own
Onion-skins preening in row.

These are signs of incontinence
Matters of low assignment.
They bring damage to us alone
No swindle to the locals
Nor incendiary to the masses
Or provocations to dissent
What we practice when at home
Nothing particular to repent.

They bring nothing to renewal
No freshening of the bed
Nor abundances of glory
Or outcroppings of song.
Where they are wrong we are wrong
The keepings of the head
Everything there's for saving
Nothing more to be said.

Desert Bloom

It's springtime in the desert
And the people throng
To watch the flowers flourish
A scrum of colors
A palette of hues
Even indigo, a blue beyond the blues
A splurge of hope and recovery
They take no mind of brevity—
The billowing colors' splash
Destined under the pounding sun
To return to its original ash
Gone until next year's return
The immensity of the desert's sands
Once held in the depths of the sea.

Like the Easter Saturday vigil
Expecting some rebirth
The congregations gather
In their defiant colors
Are bid to hold hands
And embrace across the pews
The priestly figures intercede
They look so distantly small
Choreographed in an ancient mural
Like miniatures in a play
Diminished by the ascending church walls
They bravely elevate the hosts
And daintily dab the goblets' lips

This is my body
This is my blood
Do this in remembrance

After 54 years I resume my station
And melt the dried wafer
In the heart's springtime
Ready to make my response
The answer called out of me
Remembrance
That is how I finally get it
Jesus is our study
A figure of assent
A vessel of memory
Do this …
Remembrance …
An instrument for my dead
The hope that beckons the faith
That one day we shall all come together
And stand where we have always stood
Before the burnt desert sands
And the worlds beneath the seas.

Grant it only twenty per cent of the terrain
At the maximum, thirty
That is not nothing
That is still something
A pittance of our gain
Memory and remorse are not in vain
They return us some resource
Like the desert flowers
And we join hands
Against the magnitude of sands
The never-ending space
In this time we take occasion to embrace.

The doors fly open
The voices take wing
All the choral powers
Defy the brevity of spring
Even the dead, we believe, return to sing.

A Glass of Deep Red Wine

Like a model in form
Of beauty beheld
A silken sleeved arm
Lifts a glass of deep red wine
Twirling by the light
And by the candle fire
The tumbler like a tower
With all the world in view
Tells all the bouquet
Tells all the flower
Of human desire.

It shines by dimming light
In a mosaic of flame
Against dark wood
On mirrored walls
A glass of deep red wine
Extended to sight
Tells all the taste
Tells all the glow
In human delight.

On each occasion
A glass of deep red wine
Showers the face
With radiance so ruby
It loosens the folds
Of smile and glance
All the human treasure
That throng and dance
To arouse the senses
To the gifts of pleasure.

The sibilant grace
Of a glass of deep red wine
Before the whispering blaze
Moving with measured pace
From glass to tongue
Undulations of taste
Bringing delight and desire
Whose mysteries now told
Turn flesh to living fire.

Wanderers

You cannot renege on all those years
Though unrequited and of mixed account
They come back in meinie folded
Bearing news from within and without.

Might as well push back the sky
Whose saggings inflect our every view
They are not only that which we know
Their promptings inform the ways we go.

Folk of no particular intimacy
Some of scant amiableness
Vulnerabilities must have their day
Like children peddling cookies
Knockings that can't be turned away.

With no force to gather us in
Their cards of varied appeal
Helpless if nobody's home
Or ever will be again.
They scramble to find their places.

    Vincent, raspy and gruff
    Enticing with bits of medieval lore
    Katherine, like her mother,
    Bent halfway to the floor
    John, like Fuzz, a football great
    Of more thoughtful merit
    Than blackboard teachers can claim
    Bob, dwindling down to death,
    Breaking only once to regret
    Loss of his wife's warm breath.

These are only a few
Not the most notable
Still shadowy and sparse
Whose renewal is plight
By pact I never contrived
Vagrant all these years gone
Faring a wanderer's fate
Flittings that never terminate
Only stayed by reasons of heart

Hardly themselves to maintain
They undertake their watchings
Solicitude meant our way
A selflessness so durable
A pathos without stain
Moments of wonder
Like statues in the rain

I'll do my best, I always say
It's not that easy a task
In my hard pallet and darkened hall
I sometimes tarry the call.

These beckoning apparitions
Come not tuckered,
No blood to siphon away
Or jostle at the freshing pit
It is myself they come calling about
Keeping me to a just account
These perishable goods I sustain
Are stories heard and markings sounded
Holding me to my stash and say.

Oil and Water

Master of the amber marshes,
The brown pelican, emblem of his habitat,
Drives through the wedges of the waves
Larking with the spume of sprays.
Once endangered but returned in numbers
A new strangeness cranks his toil
He is perplexed by the heavy hand
Tightly squeezing his wings
The sledge that weighs him down.
Where is the force of his former lift?
Grace actions have become obstacles
Now he staggers out of the water
And finds relief in hugging the ground.
His head dangles of a piece
Giving direction to where he falls
To rise and pierce the light no more.

Oil and water are our elements
The water that cleanses
The chrism that relumes
Oil and water extend our wings
When at baptism we are relieved
Of the soot that brought us hither
And the clothes we don
Render the soul's picture of white.
Of course this emblem cannot last
Even Jesus above the altar
Has wings distended but cannot fly
So heavy are the spikes
That drill him to the tree
Still his arms are opened wide
Ready to receive us when we too
Return to earth all darkened and stiff.

I want to go back again
When my Daddy was my Daddy
And no harm would come his way
Because I was standing by his side.
I want to go back again
When my Daddy was my Daddy
And with weapons of sharpened skill
I stood by his side.
I want to go back again
When my Daddy was my Daddy
And resting in a small bed
I sat by his side.
I want to go back again
When my Daddy was my Daddy
And lowered into the soft earth
I stood sentry by his side.

Ricardo Quinones is a scholar-critic, professor emeritus of Claremont McKenna College. He is the author of such prize-winning volumes as *The Changes of Cain: Violence and the Lost Brother in Cain-Abel Literature* (1991) and *Dualisms: The Agons of the Modern World* (2007), which was followed by *Erasmus and Voltaire: Why They Still Matter* (2010) and *North/South: The Great European Divide* (2016).

www.ingramcontent.com/pod-product-compliance
Lightning Source LLC
Chambersburg PA
CBHW050911300426
44111CB00010B/1479